WHY DOGS ARE BETTER THAN REPUBLICANS

BY J

HarperPerennial

A Division of HarperCollins*Publishers*

HarperCollins books may be purchased for
educational, business, or sales promotional use. For
information please write: Special Markets Depart-
ment, HarperCollins Publishers, Inc., 10 East 53rd Street,
New York, NY 10022.

FIRST EDITION
DESIGNED BY TOM GREENSFELDER

ISBN 0-06-092772-0
96 97 98 99 00 RRDC 10 9 8 7 6 5 4 3 2 1

BISCUITS TO THE FOLLOWING:

 MY HUMAN FAMILY: HELGA, LOUIS & DANIEL

 MY CREATURES: LYKA, ISAAC, LUCY & MAGGIE

 TOM GREENSFELDER

 TONY GARDNER — Beret

 PETERNELLE VAN ARSDALE

— RED

💡 DOUG KNOX, HOWARD GREENWICH, DAN WEISSMAN,
AMY AND WHITNEY MACDONALD, EMILY WILLIAMS,
S.L. WISENBERG, BENJAMIN LEVI, MATT MINDE,
ERIC L. TOBIAS, PEGGY FIRESTONE, JEAN RIORDAN,
NICOLE HOLLANDER, JACQUE PARSONS, BUCKY HALKER,
WOMEN & CHILDREN FIRST BOOKSTORE, DAN FRIEDMAN
(for dog sounds in foreign languages)

 ERIC BATES, MY LITTLE GENIUS

 AND, OF COURSE, TO THE REPUBLICANS FOR
MAKING THIS BOOK WRITE ITSELF. NOW GO
AWAY.

Chapter One
WHY DOGS ARE BETTER THAN REPUBLICANS

DOGS BELIEVE IN TOTAL FREEDOM OF EXPRESSION

DOGS CAN'T GET AWAY WITH BLAMING FOREIGN DOGS FOR LOCAL PROBLEMS

WOULD YOU BELIEVE THE MEXICAN HAIRLESS DID IT?

DOGS DO NOT WRAP THEMSELVES IN THE FLAG TO FURTHER THEIR OWN AGENDA

ANY **LESS** THAN EIGHT BISCUITS A DAY IS DOWNRIGHT **UNAMERICAN!**

WHILE THEY MAY FIND SOME OF IT
OFFENSIVE, DOGS SUPPORT PUBLIC
FUNDING OF THE ARTS

DOGS HAVE BETTER THINGS TO THINK ABOUT THAN CAPITAL GAINS

DOGS ARE NOT SCARED OF FEMINISTS

WHEN A DOG'S DONE WITH A TREE, IT'S STILL STANDING

DOGS ARE COMPLETELY DISINTERESTED IN YOUR SEXUALITY

BAD DOGS ARE NOT PUT ON STAMPS

DOGS THINK THE CURRICULUM COULD USE SOME EXPANSION

A DOG WOULD NEVER KEEP A DIARY DOCUMENTING ALL THE BAD THINGS HE DID

Dear Diary,
I finally figured out how to get into the trash without knocking it over! Now they'll never catch me! Then for lunch I chewed up a really nice Italian shoe....

YOU'RE ALLOWED TO STOP THE PROLIFERATION OF ILL-TEMPERED DOGS

YOU CAN STICK A DOG IN THE BACK OF
AIR FORCE ONE AND IT WON'T TRY TO SHUT
DOWN THE WHOLE GOVERNMENT IN RETALIATION

THERE'S NOTHING SCARY ABOUT YOUNG DOGS

RICH DOGS DON'T FEEL AS IF THEY
MUST BREED ONLY AMONG THEMSELVES

ILLEGAL DOG WASTE WON'T KILL YOU, AND IT DOESN'T COST MILLIONS TO CLEAN UP *

* VOID IN MANHATTAN

19

NOT ALL DOGS ARE OWNED BY CIGARETTE LOBBYISTS

DOGS VALUE THE ELDERLY, EVEN WHEN THEY REQUIRE MEDICAL CARE

DANGEROUS DOG GROUPS ARE NOT ALLOWED TO HAVE WEAPONS

DOGS ARE INTO SOLAR HEATING

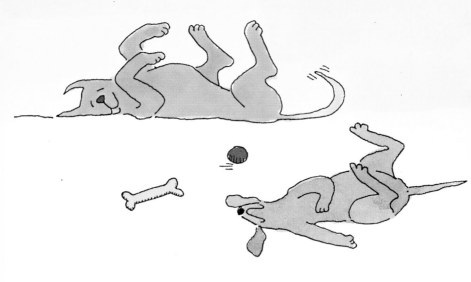

DOGS WOULD NEVER BUST A UNION

DOGS ARE LOYAL TO THEIR WORKERS

SURE, SHE HAS
HER FAULTS,
BUT SHE'S BEEN
WITH ME SINCE
I WAS WEANED~
I COULD NEVER
LET HER GO

DOGS ARE UP FRONT ABOUT THEIR AGENDA

WHEN DOGS LICK YOUR FEET, THEY DON'T EXPECT YOUR VOTE IN EXCHANGE

DOGS HAVE INTEGRITY

DOGS DON'T CHOOSE MATES BASED ON PUBLIC PERCEPTION

DOGS DON'T PRETEND TO BE WORKING CLASS WHEN THEY'RE NOT

DOGS SUPPORT FAMILY FARMS

DOGS OPPOSE THE DEATH PENALTY

FEMALE DOGS DON'T TURN ON THEIR OWN KIND

DOGS KNOW THAT FAMILIES COME IN ALL SHAPES AND SIZES

DOGS NEVER SPONSORED DEATH SQUADS IN CENTRAL AMERICA

DOGS HAVE CLEANER MOUTHS

DOGS LOVE KIDS — EVEN IF THEY HAPPEN TO BE POOR

DOGS **HELP** PEOPLE WITH DISABILITIES

DOGS ONLY WEAR THEIR OWN FUR

DOGS DON'T CARE WHAT THE OFFICIAL LANGUAGE IS

DOGS UNDERSTAND THAT "UNDEVELOPED" LAND HAS VALUE JUST AS IT IS

DOGS KNOW WHAT TO DO WITH THE "CONTRACT WITH AMERICA"

Chapter Two

WHY DOGS AND REPUBLICANS ARE THE SAME

NEITHER BELIEVES IN AUTO SAFETY

BOTH ONLY LIKE PREFERENCES WHEN THEY'RE THE ONES BEING PREFERRED

47

BOTH WANT TO TAKE SCHOOL LUNCHES AWAY FROM KIDS

NEITHER MATES FOR LIFE
(BUT DOGS DON'T PREACH ABOUT "FAMILY VALUES")

NEITHER THINKS MUCH OF THE FIRST ANIMAL

BOTH NEED TO LEARN NOT TO TAKE WHAT ISN'T THEIRS

BOTH ENJOY SHOES WITH TASSELS

BOTH WOULD PREFER TO EAT MEAT THREE TIMES A DAY

AS IN DOGS, G.O.P. YEARS × 7= ACTUAL HUMAN YEARS

THE ONES WITH FANCY PEDIGREES HAVE NO DETECTABLE BRAIN ACTIVITY

BOTH HAVE ADOPTED '60s-STYLE CIVIL DISOBEDIENCE TACTICS TO SUIT THEIR AGENDAS

BOTH HAVE INSATIABLE APPETITES FOR PORK

NEITHER UNDERSTANDS THE IMPORTANCE OF PUBLIC RADIO

NEITHER LIKES SHARING THEIR RICHES

BOTH FEEL RELIEVED WHEN THEY
CAN LET LOOSE ON RED THINGS

BOTH LIE ON COMMAND

NEITHER CAN SPELL

BOTH WANT TO INTERFERE WITH WOMEN'S REPRODUCTIVE LIVES

BOTH CAN BE BOUGHT

BOTH HAVE A PAC MENTALITY

NEITHER CARES THAT THERE'S A HOLE IN THE OZONE

A DRAMATIZATION

NEITHER KNOWS WHEN TO CHANGE THEIR HAIRDOS

Chapter Three

WHY REPUBLICANS ARE BETTER THAN DOGS

REPUBLICANS DON'T GO NUTS EVERY TIME THE DOORBELL RINGS

REPUBLICANS TEND TO HAVE TIDIER LAWNS

REPUBLICANS ONLY GET IN YOUR GARBAGE IF YOU'RE RUNNING AGAINST THEM

REPUBLICANS SOMETIMES PICK UP THE TAB

Chapter Four

WHY DOGS ARE BETTER THAN DEMOCRATS

DOGS CAN BE TRAINED TO DISTINGUISH LEFT FROM RIGHT

DOGS HAVE VERTEBRAE